peaceful jazz
piano solos
a collection of 30 pieces

ISBN 978-1-70513-253-1

Visit Hal Leonard Online at
www.halleonard.com

World headquarters, contact:
Hal Leonard
7777 West Bluemound Road
Milwaukee, WI 53213
Email: info@halleonard.com

In Europe, contact:
Hal Leonard Europe Limited
1 Red Place
London, W1K 6PL
Email: info@halleonardeurope.com

In Australia, contact:
Hal Leonard Australia Pty. Ltd.
4 Lentara Court
Cheltenham, Victoria, 3192 Australia
Email: info@halleonard.com.au

All of Me

Words and Music by Seymour Simons and Gerald Marks

All the Things You Are

from VERY WARM FOR MAY

Lyrics by Oscar Hammerstein II
Music by Jerome Kern

Angel Eyes

Words by Earl Brent
Music by Matt Dennis

Autumn Leaves

English lyric by Johnny Mercer
French lyric by Jacques Prevert
Music by Joseph Kosma

Blue Moon

Music by Richard Rodgers
Lyrics by Lorenz Hart

Body and Soul

Words by Edward Heyman, Robert Sour and Frank Eyton
Music by John Green

Easy Living

Theme from the Paramount Picture EASY LIVING

Words and Music by Leo Robin and Ralph Rainger

Easy Swing

Fly Me to the Moon

(In Other Words)

Words and Music by Bart Howard

Days of Wine and Roses

from DAYS OF WINE AND ROSES

Lyrics by Johnny Mercer
Music by Henry Mancini

Georgia on My Mind

Words by Stuart Gorrell
Music by Hoagy Carmichael

It Had to Be You

Words by Gus Kahn
Music by Isham Jones

My Romance

from JUMBO

Words by Lorenz Hart
Music by Richard Rodgers

Misty

Music by Erroll Garner

Moon River

from the Paramount Picture BREAKFAST AT TIFFANY'S

Words by Johnny Mercer
Music by Henry Mancini

Moonlight in Vermont

Words by John Blackburn
Music by Karl Suessdorf

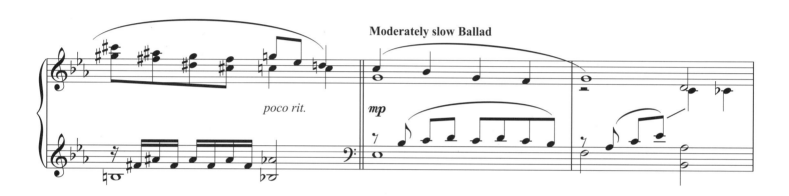

To Coda

My One and Only Love

Words by Robert Mellin
Music by Guy Wood

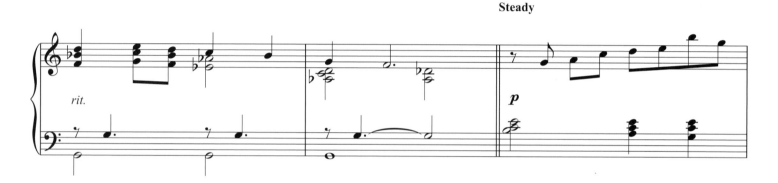

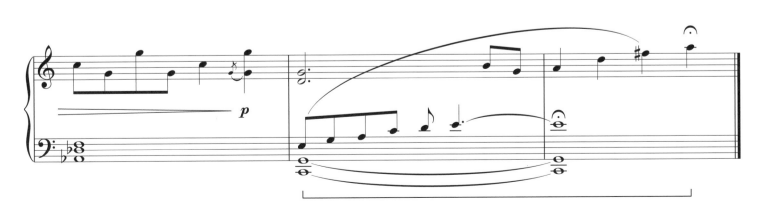

Nature Boy

Words and Music by Eden Ahbez

The Nearness of You

from the Paramount Picture ROMANCE IN THE DARK

Words by Ned Washington
Music by Hoagy Carmichael

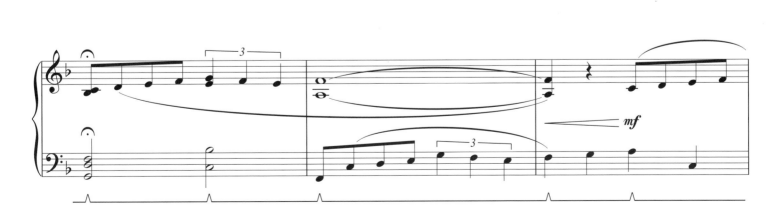

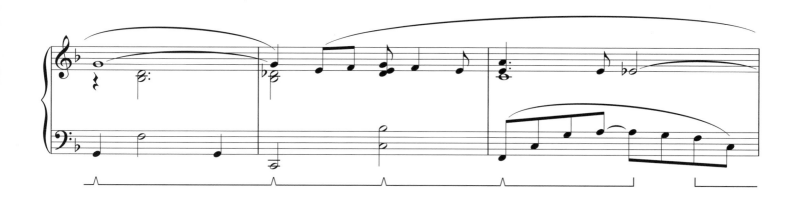

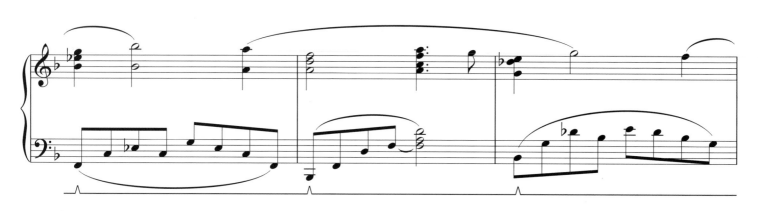

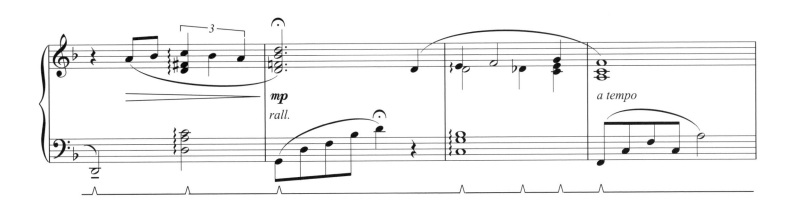

A Nightingale Sang in Berkeley Square

Lyric by Eric Maschwitz
Music by Manning Sherwin

Polka Dots and Moonbeams

Words by Johnny Burke
Music by Jimmy Van Heusen

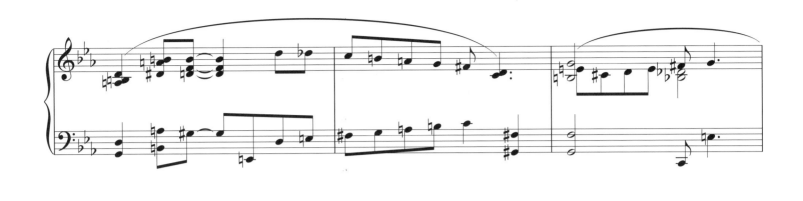

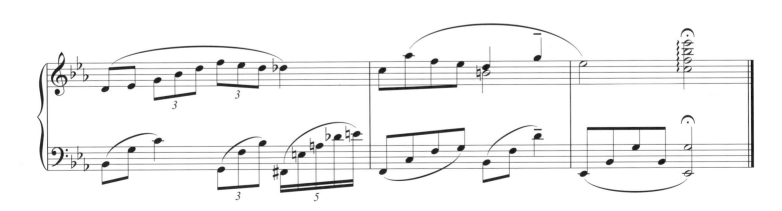

Satin Doll

By Duke Ellington

Smoke Gets in Your Eyes

from ROBERTA

Words by Otto Harbach
Music by Jerome Kern

Stardust

Words by Mitchell Parish
Music by Hoagy Carmichael

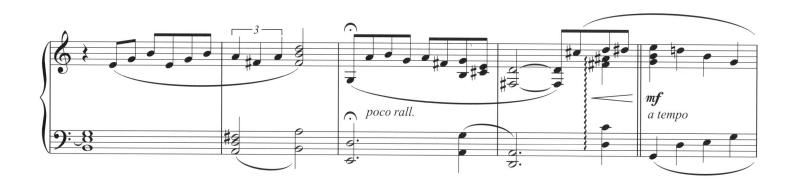

Stella By Starlight

from the Paramount Picture THE UNINVITED

By Victor Young

Summertime

from PORGY AND BESS®

Music and Lyrics by George Gershwin, DuBose and Dorothy Heyward and Ira Gershwin

The Very Thought of You

Words and Music by Ray Noble

Waltz for Debby

Lyric by Gene Lees
Music by Bill Evans

D.C. al Coda
(take 1st ending)

CODA

The Way You Look Tonight

from SWING TIME

Words by Dorothy Fields
Music by Jerome Kern

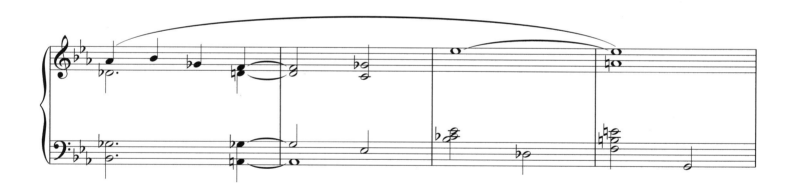

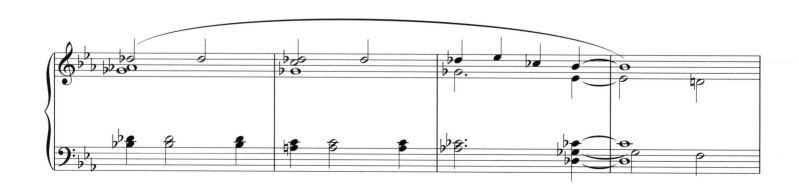

D.S. al Coda

CODA

molto rit.

a tempo

8va

When Sunny Gets Blue

Lyric by Jack Segal
Music by Marvin Fisher

What a Wonderful World

Words and Music by George David Weiss and Bob Thiele

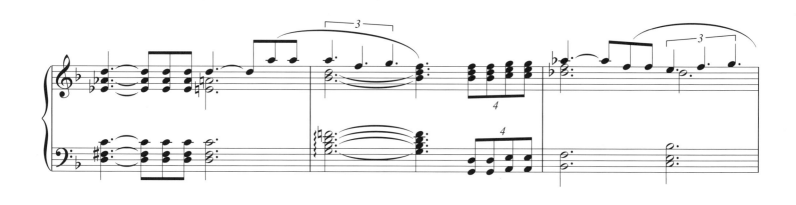

rall. e dim.